Original title:
The Strength of the Stallion

Editor: Jessica Elisabeth Luik
Author: Paulina Pähkel
ISBN HARDBACK: 978-9916-86-439-5
ISBN PAPERBACK: 978-9916-86-440-1

Boundless Power

In endless skies, the eagles soar,
With wings of might, they freely glide.
Their piercing gaze does seek and score,
The secrets in the world so wide.

Oceans roar with tidal pull,
Their depths profound, a force untamed.
In currents vast, the power's full,
To shape the shores, their will proclaimed.

Mountains rise with stern resolve,
Their peaks defy both time and storm.
Their silent strength, the rocks involve,
In nature's realm, they take their form.

Majestic Thunder

Dark clouds gather, skies contend,
The air is charged with fierce debate.
A flash, a crack, the storms extend,
Nature's voice in power state.

The rain cascades in sweeping might,
A symphony in liquid blur.
Each drop within the tempest's flight,
A part of nature's mighty stir.

The calm returns as storms retreat,
The earth renews from thunder's grace.
A testament to power's feat,
In every cloud, a fierce embrace.

Equine Majesty

In fields of green, the horses run,
Their manes aflow in morning's breeze.
With every stride beneath the sun,
They paint the land with gentle ease.

Their eyes, a window to their soul,
Reflect the boundless depths within.
A spirit wild, beyond control,
In every step, a world's begin.

Through ancient paths and meadows wide,
Their legacy in hoofbeats trace.
With strength and grace, they onward ride,
A timeless dance, a noble race.

Unyielding Spirit

In every heart, a fire burns,
A flame of dreams and hopes divine.
With every beat, the spirit turns,
To face the world with courage fine.

No storm or trial can shake the core,
Of one who stands with steadfast will.
Through night and day, they fight for more,
The silent strength they seek to fill.

A force within, unbent, unbowed,
A beacon in the darkest night.
A spirit proud, both strong and loud,
In every life, their guiding light.

Heart of Mustang

In valleys deep, where shadows lie,
A mustang runs beneath the sky.
Its heart is bold, with spirit free,
A symbol of wild sovereignty.

Through windswept plains and rugged hills,
It roams where nature's call fulfills.
With eyes that gleam like morning dew,
It carries dreams of unchained view.

In twilight's glow, it finds its grace,
A fleeting shadow, swift in pace.
Each gallop whispers tales untold,
Of ancient lands and hearts of gold.

Wind Dancer

Across the plains, where grasses sway,
A wind dancer comes out to play.
With mane untamed and wild eyes bright,
It twirls beneath the pale moonlight.

The breeze it feels, a tender touch,
That guides its limbs with grace as such.
A symphony of freedom's song,
It moves in rhythm, pure and strong.

Evening skies in hues of gold,
Embrace the dance, a sight so bold.
And in the stillness, soft and sweet,
It finds a melody complete.

Pure Wildness

Amidst the world, so vast and grand,
There's pure wildness in this land.
It courses through the veins of earth,
And gives the soul its rightful birth.

The mountains call, the rivers sing,
A primal urge to everything.
To wander free, to breathe the air,
To seek the beauty everywhere.

In every heart, a spark alive,
Of wildness pure, to feel, to thrive.
An endless dance of life unchained,
In pure wildness, truth is gained.

Trail of Courage

Through forests dense and deserts bare,
The trail of courage leads us there.
With every step, a story made,
Of battles fought and fears allayed.

The path is rough, yet spirits high,
Beneath the vast, unending sky.
Determined hearts, with eyes so strong,
They march ahead where they belong.

Each mountain climbed, each river crossed,
A testament to strength embossed.
The trail of courage, bold and true,
A journey made by the brave few.

Manes Against the Wind

Beneath the open sky so vast,
Horses race, and shadows cast.
Their manes against the wind do fly,
Like whispers of a fleeting sigh.

Graceful leaps through fields of green,
A sight so wild it's rarely seen.
Freedom calls in every stride,
With nature's pulse, they shall abide.

Hooves that pound on earth below,
In rhythmic dance, they ebb and flow.
Unbridled souls, they chase the breeze,
Finding solace among the trees.

Evening falls, yet still they run,
Chasing dreams beneath the sun.
In twilight's hush, they find their rest,
Manes still flowing, wild and blessed.

Indomitable Spirit

In the heart of every storm,
Lies a spirit, warm and warm.
Undeterred by fear or fright,
Burning with an endless light.

Mountains rise and oceans swell,
Yet this spirit stands so well.
Trials come and shadows loom,
Still, it blossoms, ever bloom.

Strength is found in every scar,
Guided by its northern star.
With each challenge, it ascends,
Finding courage, never bends.

Hands that lift the fallen ones,
Hearts that shine like morning suns.
Indomitable it remains,
Breaking free from all the chains.

Storm Chaser

Chasing clouds across the sky,
Where thunder roars and eagles fly.
Riding winds to worlds unknown,
In the storm, they feel at home.

Eyes of steel, they pierce the night,
With every flash, they see the light.
Roaring winds and blazing skies,
Their playground where the tempest lies.

Wave on wave, the fury builds,
Yet they glide through distant fields.
Dancing with the hurricane,
Never held by fear or chain.

Lightning paints their path so bright,
Guiding them through darkest night.
Storm chasers with hearts so bold,
Stories of the storm are told.

The Untamed Gallop

Fields of golden hues and green,
Where wilderness feels so serene.
Their spirits rise with every leap,
In freedom's arms, their souls shall keep.

Through valleys deep and mountains high,
Their call is found where eagles fly.
Untamed gallop, wild and free,
A testament to liberty.

No reins to bind, nor fences hold,
Their tales of freedom softly told.
Nature's guardians, proud and true,
Running where the skies are blue.

In every gust, in every breeze,
Their essence floats with leafy trees.
Untamed gallop through the land,
In harmony, they understand.

Running the Ridge

The wind beneath my soles,
Across the ridge I glide,
With earth's ancient scrolls,
Nature as my guide.

Mountains whisper bold,
Secrets pure and true,
Stories yet untold,
In the morning dew.

Each step a dancer's grace,
Over stones and leaves,
In this sacred space,
Heart and soul it weaves.

Ridge lines paint the sky,
Horizons far and wide,
Where dreams and spirits fly,
With no place to hide.

Echoes in the Canyon

Whispers through the vale,
Ancient voices sing,
In the canyon's tale,
Where memories cling.

Shadows dance on walls,
Songs of time gone by,
Nature's humble halls,
Underneath the sky.

River's gentle sigh,
In the canyon deep,
Stars in silent cry,
Eternal secrets keep.

Mountains guard the lore,
Echoes call my name,
In the canyon's core,
I am but a flame.

Free Spirit's Journey

Footprints on the sand,
Waves kiss the shore,
Journey to a land,
I've never seen before.

Stars my only guide,
In the night's embrace,
Through the great divide,
A timeless, open space.

Mountains bow so low,
Whispering their grace,
Where free spirits flow,
In nature's warm embrace.

Fields of endless green,
Sky so vast and blue,
Where my soul has been,
I'll return anew.

Night's Sentinel

Underneath the moon,
Shadows come to play,
In the night's dark tune,
Silent wolves do bay.

Stars above so bright,
Guardians of the night,
In their silver light,
Dreams take silent flight.

Quiet sentinel,
Tree and rock and stream,
Keep the secrets well,
Of the night's soft dream.

Dawn breaks gently through,
Night must fade away,
Sentinel bids adieu,
To the new-born day.

Courage Reins

Within the storm, a heart does beat,
Against the wind, it won't retreat.
In shadows thick, it finds the spark,
To light the way when all seems dark.

Through valleys low and mountains tall,
It answers every daunting call.
Resilient as the ancient oak,
Courage reigns, fear is broke.

When all are lost in disarray,
A steadfast soul will find its way.
With every step, and every fight,
Courage shines, a guiding light.

Wild Harmony

In fields of green where rivers flow,
Nature's symphony does gently grow.
A wild harmony, sweet and fierce,
Binding realms it deftly pierce.

Birds above in joyous flight,
Stars at rest through the night.
Waves of leaves in breezes play,
Wild harmony leads the way.

Through tangled woods and open space,
It weaves a tune, a soft embrace.
Echoes of a song pristine,
Wild harmony stands serene.

Trail of Strength

Upon the path where heroes tread,
Through trials where the bold have led.
A trail of strength, carved in stone,
Whispers of the great unknown.

Each footfall tells a tale unsung,
Every climb, a victory won.
Through hardship's fire, tempers steel,
A trail of strength, minds reveal.

In the dust, the spirit learns,
As the earth beneath it turns.
With every stride, it grows anew,
A trail of strength, pure and true.

Fierce Elegance

In silent grace, it takes the stage,
A melding of the calm and rage.
Fierce elegance, a sight to see,
A dance of power, wild yet free.

With every move, a story told,
In fierce elegance, spirits bold.
Waves of strength with gentle sway,
A balance wrought in life's display.

Through the chaos, it remains,
A beauty that the world sustains.
In every heart, a quiet flame,
Fierce elegance, ever the same.

Wilderness Pioneer

Beneath the ancient canopy,
Through pathways wild and free,
He treads where none have dared,
In nature's grand decree.

With compass heart aligned,
And spirit unconfined,
The whispers of the trees,
In harmony entwined.

The rivers weave his tale,
As stars above unveil,
A lone explorer's dream,
On destiny's bold trail.

His courage never bends,
In shadows, he ascends,
The wilderness, his stage,
Where every journey ends.

A testament to will,
Through valleys, over hill,
The pioneer commands,
His legend lingers still.

Eternal Gallop

Through fields of endless green,
A horse with spirit keen,
Forever gallops free,
In twilight's serene sheen.

The wind beneath his mane,
No reins to bind or chain,
He races with the sun,
Where time cannot explain.

Hooves beat a timeless rhyme,
A dance with ancient time,
Each heartbeat echoes life's,
Indomitable climb.

In moonlit meadows deep,
Where silent shadows creep,
His journey never ends,
These dreams forever keep.

Eternal in his stride,
With stars that will not hide,
A symbol of the wild,
By nature's laws, he's tied.

Savannah's Guardian

Beneath the golden sun,
Where life and silence run,
A guardian stands true,
Savannah's chosen one.

His eyes survey the land,
With wisdom's gentle hand,
Protecting wild and free,
In harmony, they stand.

The whisper of the grass,
As clouded shadows pass,
He knows each secret name
That nature shall amass.

Through drought and evening rains,
He guards the endless plains,
A sentinel of peace,
Where life's pure spirit reigns.

His heart, a steadfast beat,
In rhythms wild and sweet,
The savannah's soul he keeps,
Beneath his watchful feet.

Steadfast Charger

In armor shining bright,
Through darkest day and night,
The charger rides with pride,
A symbol of the fight.

His heart fearless and bold,
A spirit uncontrolled,
He gallops through the fray,
With legends yet untold.

No challenge makes him yield,
On battlefield or field,
Steadfast, he stands his ground,
A sword that none can wield.

Through storm and tempest wild,
His journey undefiled,
A beacon in the dark,
For hope, he's reconciled.

Upon the winds of fate,
Through history's open gate,
The steadfast charger rides,
Eternal, strong, and great.

Legendary Hooves

Upon the plains, where shadows lie,
Hooves beat strong, a song to sky.
Myths and tales borne in stride,
Legends breathe, where spirits bide.

Golden fields beneath the moon,
Echoes chant a timeless tune.
Hear the thunder, wild and free,
In each step, eternity.

Ancient paths they carve anew,
Mysteries in cadence true.
Every hoofprint tells a story,
Of untamed lands, eternal glory.

Rider's Pride

In the reins, the power flows,
Between the hearts, a bond that grows.
Through the storm, and through the sun,
Together fierce, together one.

The world unfolds beyond their sight,
In every gallop, pure delight.
Whispered secrets, shared and known,
Where rider's pride is clearly shown.

Unseen currents guide their way,
As night gives birth to break of day.
Their silhouettes, a dance of joy,
Inseparable, no force could cloy.

Bold Horizon

Eyes set firm on distant gleam,
Beyond what waking eyes have seen.
Mountains rise and rivers flow,
Toward horizons bold we go.

Each sunrise paints a tale unsung,
Of courage found and dreams begun.
In every stride, the quest is near,
No shadow casts a hint of fear.

Adventure calls from every peak,
Unknown paths the bold shall seek.
With every dawn, a promise new,
Horizon whispers, 'Follow through.'

Essence of Resistance

In the quiet moments of despair,
Strength arises, thin as air.
From the cracks, a burgeon blooms,
As hope dispels the darkest glooms.

Against the tide, resolve will hold,
In whispered winds, defiance bold.
Every challenge met with grace,
A spark of fire in every face.

With each fall, the spirit soars,
Breaking through unseen doors.
Resistance grows with every breath,
A testament to life through death.

Sunset Charge

Crimson hues the sky ignites,
Mountains bask in twilight's glow.
Shadows stretch as day takes flight,
Whispers dance where breezes flow.

Bronze-lit waves crash on the shore,
Echoes of the sun's retreat.
Nature's symphony does soar,
Twilight's call, serene, discreet.

Horses gallop 'cross the plains,
Silhouettes in evening's blush.
Freedom courses through their veins,
Night descends, the world is hush.

Stars awaken, twilight's kin,
Each one tells a tale of old.
Dreams begin where day has been,
Mysteries in starlight scrolled.

In the dusk, we find our grace,
Lost in colors, bold, profound.
Under heaven's vast embrace,
Peace in sunset's charge is found.

In the Dust's Embrace

Desert winds, a whisper's trace,
In the dust, our story's spun.
Footprints lost, an endless race,
Beneath the blazing, scorching sun.

Cacti stand as silent guards,
Sentinels of ancient days.
Life persists in harsh regards,
Thriving in the sun's harsh rays.

Mirages dance on distant sands,
Illusions of an oasis near.
Hope persists in barren lands,
Faith endures through trials severe.

Night descends, the sky aflame,
Stars ignite the sable dome.
Dreams arise from where we came,
Found within the desert's poem.

In the dust, our souls take flight,
Boundless skies our hearts embrace.
Journey's path, both day and night,
Strength is found in dust's embrace.

Field's Bravest

Morning mist on dewy fields,
Whispers of the dawn unfold.
Battle cries, the heart congeals,
Echoes of the brave and bold.

Armor glints in the first light,
Champions face the breaking day.
Courage stirred, the fire ignite,
Marching forth without delay.

Victory lies in each stride,
Honored vows they tightly hold.
In their hearts, no fear will bide,
Legends of the field retold.

Though the shadows may advance,
Stand they firm, resolve anew.
In the dance of fate's cruel chance,
Valor's light is shining through.

Heroes rise from common ground,
Strengthened by the trials faced.
In the field, where glories found,
Echoes of the bravest traced.

Trailblazer's Fury

Mountains quiver, forest roars,
A path forged in fervent haste.
Rivers cut through ancient floors,
Nature's power left untraced.

Blazing trails with might and will,
Ventures led by daring hearts.
Seekers of the unknown thrill,
Drawing maps in wildest arts.

Thunder cracks in distant skies,
Heralds of the storm's embrace.
Charged with fury, tempest rise,
Leading on at breakneck pace.

Valleys echo with their shouts,
Triumph in the face of fear.
In the wild, through twisting routes,
Pioneers of frontiers clear.

Trailblazers carve history's tale,
Legacy in earth's embrace.
Through the tempest, winds they sail,
With a fury none replace.

Guardian of the Meadow

In the blush of dawn's first light,
A sentinel stands, so bright.
Whispers through the waking grass,
Bear tales of nights that pass.

Silent watch with eyes so keen,
Over fields of endless green.
A heart that beats with nature's song,
In the meadow, where dreams belong.

Clouds drift by, an endless scroll,
Echoes of the earth's own soul.
Boundaries dissolve to none,
Beneath the early morning sun.

Peaceful is the humble guard,
Unscarred by struggle, unbarred.
With every rustling leaf and breeze,
He remains, the meadow's peace.

Evening comes, the stars afire,
A vigil carried, never tired.
Guardian 'neath the moon's soft glow,
In the meadow, all things grow.

Unyielding Companion

Through tempest wild and calmest seas,
A friend who stands, unbent, at ease.
Strength and solace side by side,
In such a bond, we both confide.

Pages turned as years go past,
A steadfast shadow ever cast.
Through laughter bright and sorrow's tear,
A presence constant, ever near.

No storm can take, no tide can break,
What we give and what we take.
In the tapestry of time's own thread,
Together still, paths we tread.

In darkest night and light of day,
An anchor true, a guiding ray.
With whispers kind, and silence loud,
We walk our paths, heads unbowed.

Unyielding as the mountain's height,
A bond that glowing embers light.
Companion through both joy and strife,
In every breath, we share this life.

Majesty on Four Legs

In the forest's ancient shade,
Graceful steps by nature made.
Eyes that pierce through twilight's shroud,
Silent prayer, nobly vowed.

Every movement speaks of grace,
Wilderness as sacred space.
With whispered wind and fallen leaf,
A monarch's reign, beyond belief.

Golden fur or midnight hue,
Companion of the old and new.
Bearer of the wild's refrain,
Untamed spirit, boundless reign.

Silent paths where shadows blend,
Majesty with no end.
Heartbeats echo, beating time,
Nature's throne in form divine.

In the tale that trees have told,
Legends of the brave and bold.
Majesty on four legs free,
Sovereign spirit, wild decree.

Wind's Favorite

In the dance of leaves and sky,
Where the breezes laugh and sigh.
Swift and light through branches weave,
A story that the winds believe.

Whispers carried far and wide,
On the back of zephyrs ride.
Secrets from the mountaintops,
Where the wind's own heart never stops.

Soft caresses, storms that roar,
Songs of ages evermore.
Traveler through realms unseen,
Winds of wanderlust, serene.

Through the grasses, wild and free,
Wind's own muse, in sweet decree.
Every rise and every fall,
In the breath of nature call.

With each gust that intertwines,
Softly, wind's favorite binds.
Echoes of the earth's own breath,
In the dance of life and death.

Nature's Warrior

In the heart of the forest, green and deep,
A warrior of nature takes his leap.
Among the trees, where secrets lie,
He whispers dreams to the open sky.

With courage drawn from roots so old,
His spirit dances, brave and bold.
Leaves caress with every stride,
In nature's realm, he won't hide.

Through the thicket and the dappled shade,
He finds the path that time has made.
Silent guardian of all that's pure,
In his hands, the forest's cure.

From dawn to dusk, he stands his ground,
Where echoes of life are the only sound.
In the circle of life, his endless fight,
Nature and he, forever tight.

Under moon's glow, or sun's bright flame,
His quest and honor stay the same.
Nature's warrior, strong and free,
Bound to the wild, eternally.

Among the Herd

In fields of green, where shadows play,
Among the herd, I find my way.
A unity in every stride,
A bond with nature we can't hide.

From dawn to dusk, in line we'll roam,
Togetherness becomes our home.
Side by side, we tread the land,
At peace with life, we understand.

The whispers of the wind we chase,
In harmony, we find our place.
The call of wild, the scents so real,
Among the herd, we find and feel.

Strength in numbers, hearts as one,
Beneath the sky, beneath the sun.
In a tapestry of earth's grand scheme,
Together we live, together we dream.

With each hoofbeat, a story told,
Among the herd, both young and old.
Lessons of life, in every glance,
A sacred dance, a timeless trance.

Freedom's Champion

In open fields where wild winds blow,
A champion of freedom begins to show.
Their heart as vast as the endless sky,
They lift their wings, prepared to fly.

Through valleys deep and towering heights,
They embrace their endless flights.
Bound by nothing, free as light,
Their spirit shines both day and night.

A herald of dreams and soaring hopes,
They navigate life's varied slopes.
Unshackled by the chains of fear,
To far horizons, they draw near.

In the embrace of the heavens wide,
They ride the currents, they can't hide.
With every breath, with every beat,
Freedom courses through their feet.

An emblem of what it means to be,
Unchained, untamed, forever free.
In every step, in every flight,
Freedom's champion, pure delight.

Running with Shadows

In the twilight's hush, where the shadows play,
A figure runs at the close of day.
Silent steps on paths unknown,
In the realm where starlight's shown.

A dance with shadows, smooth and fast,
In every move, an echo of the past.
Through whispering trees and moonlit lanes,
Freedom flows within their veins.

Draped in mystery, cloaked in night,
They find their way by silver light.
With shadows as their constant friend,
The journey's start, without an end.

In the stillness of the evening air,
They cast their hopes without a care.
Though shadows stretch and grow so tall,
They embrace the night, they heed the call.

Running with shadows, bold and free,
In the darkness, they come to see.
A world of dreams, a way to be,
In the dance of shadows, they find the key.

Boundless Energy

In dawn's first light, they rise anew,
With spirits high, the day is fresh,
Every stride a heartbeat's echo,
A dance of life, vibrant and rash.

Over fields of emerald green,
Through the whispers of the breeze,
They gallop free, a sight unseen,
Nature's chorus, wild and pleased.

Their limbs in sync, a force profound,
Unbridled power, taut and sleek,
A storm in motion, thunder's sound,
In their eyes, the endless peak.

Each leap, each bound, a story told,
Of strength and grace entwined,
With hearts of fire, pure and bold,
In their freedom, beauty find.

For in their veins runs energy,
Unfettered by the binds of time,
A testament to liberty,
In every running rhyme.

Majesty in Motion

Amid the plains, a regal stride,
Majestic in their silent grace,
With mane and tail as flags implied,
In twilight's soft, embracing space.

The golden dusk reflects their sheen,
As day meets night in subtle blend,
Their every move, serene, pristine,
An artistry with no pretend.

The sway of grass, their fleeting mark,
A gentle rhythm, soul's embrace,
In every hoofbeat, echoes hark,
Of primal strength, of ancient place.

Through rivers' edge and forest's bend,
Their spirits wander, wild and free,
Upon their path, no tether's end,
For in their freedom, destiny.

They are the essence of the earth,
Embodied pride, untamed and true,
In them, the world's eternal birth,
Majesty in motion's view.

Legacy of Hooves

Upon the hills, their lineage runs,
With echoes of a time long past,
In shadows cast by setting suns,
Their legacy in hooves is vast.

With every step, they weave a tale,
Of ancestors who roamed the plains,
Through storm and calm, through wind and hail,
In their steps, the past remains.

The old paths crossed, they trace anew,
In whispers of the tall, green grass,
With eyes that see the world so true,
The future and the eras pass.

From foal to steed, the lesson taught,
Of wanderlust and strength's embrace,
In every stride, no destiny sought,
But freedom, in its purest grace.

For they are more than just their form,
They are the breaths of history,
In every pulse, in every storm,
Lives the legacy of hooves set free.

Eclipsing Horizons

With eyes set on the farthest line,
Where sky and earth converge to kiss,
They run where dreams and hopes combine,
In that ethereal, boundless bliss.

Their shadows stretch at day's retreat,
Chasing the sun's last, glowing thread,
A race that time cannot defeat,
Where future and the past are wed.

Beneath the vast, unending skies,
Their forms a silhouette of grace,
Eclipsing horizons in their rise,
A journey to an unknown place.

Each heartbeat syncs with earth below,
In harmony with nature's plan,
Through every landscape's ebb and flow,
They chart the legacy of man.

For in their stride, a tale unfolds,
Of boundless courage, wild and grand,
Eclipsing horizons as life molds,
A testament of hoof and land.

Valley Strider

In valleys green, where rivers flow,
Beneath the sky's cerulean glow,
A strider moves with silent grace,
Through nature's vast, unending space.

Each step a whisper, soft and light,
A shadow in the morning light,
Amongst the trees and emerald hills,
Where time itself in peace distills.

Mountains watch his fearless path,
Unmoved by storm or winter's wrath,
With every stride, his spirit free,
In harmony with earth and sea.

A life of roam, a journey long,
His heart beats like a timeless song,
In valleys deep, he finds his way,
A wanderer, both night and day.

Stars will guide his endless quest,
Through lands of wonder, east to west,
A strider wandering through the vale,
Where dreams and whispers weave a tale.

Untamed Valor

Beneath the storm, in thunder's roar,
A heart that dares and yearns for more,
Untamed and fierce, with valor bright,
Embraces dark, yet seeks the light.

Eyes that gleam with fire's blaze,
In wild terrain, they boldly gaze,
No chain or shackle holds this soul,
In freedom's quest, they find their goal.

Through tempests wild and rough terrain,
The spirit never bends to pain,
With courage vast, they stride ahead,
Where fear would cower, they instead.

Each challenge met with roaring pride,
In nature's wrath, they find their stride,
Untamed by fate, they carve their way,
And revel in the break of day.

A legacy in winds they've sown,
Of strength and will, forever known,
Untamed in heart, with valor pure,
Their path of legend will endure.

Noble Raider

Upon the steed, the rider grand,
Through heated dunes and desert sand,
With noble heart and spirit's flame,
They ride to forge a timeless name.

Underneath the sun's harsh glare,
Their courage sings through torrid air,
A figure proud, with banner high,
As swift as eagle in the sky.

Through battles fierce and trials bold,
Their story, ancient, yet retold,
With every raid, their legend grows,
In whispered tales that the wind bestows.

From mount to shore, their journey led,
By honor's code and firm tread,
With noble cause, they forge their fate,
Through dawn and dusk, they never wait.

The paths they ride, with purpose true,
In endless night or morning dew,
Their legacy, by moon or star,
Will echo near, will travel far.

Inexorable Hoofbeats

In night's embrace and day's bright gleam,
The sound of hooves like twilight's dream,
Pounding earth with rhythmic might,
A force that rides past dawn to night.

Through forest dense and open plain,
Their beat resounds like steady rain,
An endless surge, a pulse of time,
On stony path or hill they climb.

Relentless stride and tireless pace,
Inexorable, they find their place,
Beneath the moon and sun's bold gaze,
Through bitter cold or summer's blaze.

Each gallop, echo of a vow,
Unbroken heart, yet to bow,
The hoofbeats carry dreams untold,
In timeless dance, both fierce and bold.

Wherever shadows mark their trail,
Through stormy skies or gentle gale,
The hoofbeats lead, in ceaseless quest,
To lands unknown, the wildest west.

Foreshadowed Victory

The dawn whispers of dreams to come,
In shadows deep, the battles won.
A warrior's heart, steadfast and true,
Awaits the sun, the morning's hue.

With every step, resolve does grow,
The path ahead, where legends flow.
Whispers linger, fate's decree,
In silent echoes, victory.

Eyes aflame with distant sight,
In darkened hours, the guiding light.
A promise held in twilight's breath,
The dawn unveiled, defying death.

Through trials harsh, the spirit soars,
Unyielding faith, forever more.
In whispered winds, the tale unfolds,
A victory, in hearts it holds.

The final crest, the summit near,
In silence loud, the end is clear.
A foreshadowed dawn, a victory,
In whispered dreams, eternally.

Galloping Glory

Fields of green, the stallions ride,
In open plains, with strength and pride.
Hooves thunder as the earth does quake,
In galloping glory, trails they make.

A bond unspoken, rider and steed,
Together bound, in hearts they heed.
Through rivers swift and mountains tall,
Their spirits rise, they never fall.

In dawn's first light, their journey starts,
With pounding hooves and fervent hearts.
Each moment passed, a fleeting song,
In galloping glory, swift and strong.

Windswept manes in morning's hue,
The world a blur, the distance blue.
In unity, their destinies intertwine,
In endless chase of the horizon line.

The sun dips low, a golden sea,
In twilight's grasp, they still run free.
In shadows cast by setting sun,
Their galloping glory, never done.

Wind-Sculpted Hero

In rugged cliffs where eagles soar,
A hero's tale heard evermore.
Carved by winds and time's decree,
A legend born 'neath sky and sea.

The whispering zephyrs, secrets share,
Of valor found in tempest air.
In storm's embrace, they rise anew,
A figure bold, both tried and true.

The elements shape their destiny,
Through trials harsh, they seek to be.
A testament to nature's might,
In wild winds, they find their light.

Mountains high and valleys low,
Each step they take, the legends grow.
In every breeze, their spirit shown,
A wind-sculpted hero, strength unknown.

When twilight falls and night is near,
Their echoes cast, both far and clear.
In timeless winds, their tales abide,
A hero forged where wild winds ride.

One with the Horizon

At daybreak's cusp, a journey starts,
With endless dreams and restless hearts.
The sun ascends, the quest begun,
To find the place where sky meets sun.

Through desert sands and forests deep,
With stars as guides, in night they'd creep.
Each horizon, a promise new,
Of worlds beyond, in distant hue.

The horizon calls in whispered tones,
A siren's song in undertones.
In every dawn, a tale reborn,
In twilight's grace, the dreams adorn.

One step leads to another year,
A path unseen, yet always clear.
With eyes afixed to distant skies,
They chase the edge where freedom lies.

In unity, they roam and soar,
With hearts that seek the evermore.
Together bound, yet free to roam,
One with the horizon, always home.

Fierce Symphony

A storm brews in the night sky,
Thunder roars, lightning twirls by,
Nature's orchestra, wild and free,
Playing a fierce, untamed symphony.

Waves crash upon the rocky shore,
Echoes of power, ancient lore,
The wind's howl becomes a mighty cry,
A symphony that will never die.

Trees dance in the tempest's embrace,
Leaves swirl in a frantic race,
Each note of the storm, full of grace,
An aria that time cannot erase.

Mountains stand, shadows cast long,
Amidst the chaos, forever strong,
The earth rumbles with the song,
A fierce symphony where all belong.

At dawn, the skies will clear,
Leaving behind echoes so dear,
Nature's voice, loud and sincere,
A symphony for the fearless to hear.

Wind's Champion

High above the fields do they soar,
Wings spread wide, yearning for more,
The wind's champion, forever bold,
A story in the sky, untold.

Mountains call to their fleeting flight,
Through the valleys, day or night,
Defying gravity, swift and light,
The horizon's edge, a boundless sight.

Across oceans deep and vast,
Whispers of legends from the past,
Every gust, a steadfast cast,
In the wind's arms, their fate is fast.

Feathers glisten in the solar hue,
Through storm and calm, they construe,
The wind's champion, strong and true,
In skies of gray or vibrant blue.

When twilight falls, their tales remain,
Echoed in the wind's soft refrain,
A dance of courage, without restrain,
Ephemeral, yet eternally ingrained.

Banner of the Wild

In forests deep where shadows hide,
A banner flutters, side by side,
With whispers of the ancient lore,
Guardians of the wild's core.

Branches sway in a silent cheer,
For those who hold the wild dear,
A chorus born from leaf and vine,
A banner that will always shine.

Rivers weave a silver line,
Through meadows rich with tales divine,
Nature's tapestry, bold and bright,
A banner raised in pure delight.

Mountains rise against the sky,
Clouds part, and eagles fly,
With every beat of heart so mild,
They hold the banner of the wild.

From dawn's light to twilight's shroud,
Nature sings her anthem loud,
And in each heart, forever filed,
Lives the banner of the wild.

Champions of the Open

Beneath the sky, so wide, unbound,
Champions stand on sacred ground,
Where freedom's breath is all around,
To nature's call, their hearts are wound.

In deserts vast with golden sands,
Or verdant fields where rivers expand,
They walk the open, strong and grand,
With dreams as boundless as the land.

Through canyons carved by ancient hands,
And forests where the great oaks stand,
They journey forth, the Earth's command,
Unified by a brave, silent band.

Ocean waves beneath the moon's glow,
Mountains capped with pure white snow,
The open calls, and they will go,
Champions of a world they know.

Each step they take, with spirits free,
In open spaces, wild and free,
Their legacy, a roaming spree,
Champions of the open sea.

Echoes of the Plains

Whispers in the wind so soft,
Carry tales of days afar.
Sunset paints the golden loft,
Underneath a rising star.

Cattle roam the grassy seas,
Guided by the herder's call.
Ancient oaks and busy bees,
Witness seasons rise and fall.

Wildflowers dot the open field,
Petals woven like a quilt.
Nature's beauty, unconcealed,
In her, endless marvels built.

Larks and sparrows serenade,
Skyward, they perform their song.
In the plains, old memories fade,
Yet new dreams are born along.

Yet as twilight meets the dawn,
Shadows cast and gently wanes.
Life goes on, the world moves on,
Echoes still within the plains.

Force of Nature

Thunder roars across the sky,
Lightning cracks a brilliant white.
Mighty winds begin to cry,
Nature's power, bold and bright.

Rivers carve their ancient paths,
Mountains stand their endless guard.
Life in all its forms amass,
From land and sea, it's never marred.

Forests thick with earthy scent,
Whisper secrets old and vast.
Creatures of the night present,
Echoes of a timeless past.

Seasons turn with steadfast grace,
Winter, Spring, and Summer's might.
Autumn leaves fall into place,
Completing nature's endless flight.

Infinite as ocean's blue,
Force of Nature fierce, profound.
In its arms, both wild and true,
Life's eternal roots are found.

Wildfire in the Canyon

Flames that dance beneath the night,
Licking shadows on the wall.
Canyon's breath ignites the sight,
Nature's fury, nature's call.

Trees stand firm in glowing blaze,
Crunch of leaves beneath the blaze.
Flickering lights in orange haze,
In the twilight's tangled maze.

Smoke curls up in spiral waves,
Stars look on from heights above.
Silence in the fire's embrace,
Conflicting with the world of love.

Creatures flee the burning path,
Instinct guiding every turn.
In the wake of nature's wrath,
Lessons learned in flames that burn.

Morning breaks and all is still,
Ashes fall like gentle snow.
Canyon breathes, it always will,
Cycles of the wild will grow.

Silver Lightning

Silver streaks across the dark,
Pierce the veil of night with gleam.
Thunder's drum, a mighty arc,
Echoes through a waking dream.

Clouds that churn and roil with might,
Skies alight with purest force.
Nature's canvas, painted bright,
Storm's the guide; it's charted course.

Rainfall cools the heated earth,
Drops like diamonds from the sky.
With each flash, a rebirth,
Bringing life to lands once dry.

Mountains tremble in the wake,
Power surging, nature's breath.
Every bolt a path to make,
Clearing, cleansing, no regret.

Night turns day with blinding streak,
Silver lightning, fierce and wild.
In its beauty, awe we seek,
Nature's force, both grand and mild.

Eternal Ride

In twilight's gentle, amber glow,
Where shadows dance, the rivers flow,
Two souls embark on paths unknown,
Through whispers of the winds, they've grown.

With stars to guide and moon to light,
They venture forth into the night,
An endless quest, a heartfelt flight,
Together braving darkest fright.

The journey long, yet paths remain,
In heartbeats shared, in love's refrain,
Through storms and sun, through joy and pain,
Their souls entwined in endless chain.

The world expands in hues untold,
With every step, as days unfold,
A tale of ages, brave and bold,
In dreams, their destinies behold.

In twilight's hue, their spirits bide,
On trails they trod, with hearts as guide,
Forevermore, they'll side by side,
Embrace the world on the eternal ride.

Stalwart Journey

With courage firm and vision clear,
Through valleys deep, o'er mountains sheer,
A steadfast heart, they persevere,
Their spirits high, no room for fear.

The winding roads and paths unknown,
In unity, they've always grown,
Through tales of hope, in whispers sown,
As seeds of dreams, they've freshly flown.

Their journey steadfast, forward strides,
With strength they face the changing tides,
In every trial, their bond abides,
Through all of life, their hearts as guides.

With every dawn and new sunrise,
Through vibrant fields and azure skies,
The bond that keeps their spirits wise,
A never-ending, grand surprise.

Onward they go, with heads held high,
Through times of joy, through times they cry,
Their journey scripts 'neath endless sky,
A stalwart path, till worlds comply.

Symbols of Might

In realms of old, where legends lie,
With banners high against the sky,
A sigil bold, a battle cry,
Their symbols mark where fates defy.

Eleven hearts, with strength they stand,
In unity, they guard the land,
With swords and shields in steadfast hand,
Through shadows deep, by fate's command.

Each emblem tells a story grand,
Of battles fought on glistening sand,
Of heroes brave who took a stand,
In echoes broad, they still expand.

The crests and marks of valor bright,
In midnight's glow, in morning light,
A saga from an age of might,
Their spirit soaring, taking flight.

So stand they proud, with symbols raised,
In honor bound, their glory praised,
A legacy through time amazed,
In hearts, their strength forever blazed.

Majestic Equine Power

With manes that flow and hooves that pound,
In fields of green, their strength unbound,
The equine grace, with beauty crowned,
In nature's court, they reign profound.

Their gallop swift, through winds they glide,
Across the plains, with none to chide,
In harmony, with Earth allied,
Majestic souls, their spirit wide.

Their eyes, a gateway to the free,
Reflect the skies, the dreams, the sea,
In silent strength, their legacy,
A symbol vast of liberty.

Through ancient lore, through modern days,
Their power shines in countless ways,
A bond with man, in dance and praise,
A testament to nature's blaze.

In every stride, in every leap,
Their majesty through hearts will seep,
In timeless grace, their essence deep,
A promise true, forever keep.

Ironclad Maverick

In the forge of dreams, undaunted heart,
Battles fierce, where shadows dart.
A lone star shines amidst the fray,
Ironclad maverick, leads the way.

With steadfast gaze, in tempest walks,
Tales of bravery, each scar talks.
Guarded by a will of steel,
Defying fate with every heel.

On the precipice of doubt, he stands,
Charting paths in unknown lands.
Bound by honor, not by chain,
Every loss, an endless gain.

Echoes of valor, in silence sung,
History's threads, by deeds strung.
Forge anew, a brighter flame,
Unyielding soul, ever the same.

When twilight cloaks the golden sky,
His legacy will never die.
Ironclad maverick, timeless lore,
Through ages past, forevermore.

Grace Under Fire

Amidst the rage of embers bright,
She walks with grace, in flickered light.
Unwavering calm, in chaos finds,
Searing trials, a tempered mind.

Beneath the heat, where others fall,
Her spirit soars, unbound by thrall.
In every spark, reflections gleam,
Unyielding strength, fuels her dream.

Through storms of flame, she charts her course,
With silent might and gentle force.
Her grace a shield, her heart a fire,
Each breath a hymn, of pure desire.

When fear encroaches, dark and cold,
She stands undaunted, fierce and bold.
Her presence, like a seraph's wing,
In midst of trials, she learns to sing.

Grace under fire, a beacon bright,
In darkest times, her guiding light.
A tapestry of strength and love,
Beneath the stars, and skies above.

In the Path of Legends

Tread softly where legends once did walk,
In shadowed realms, where stories talk.
Their echoes whisper through the night,
Guiding dreams in silent flight.

With footsteps traced in ancient dust,
They left behind a sacred trust.
In every deed, a tale unfolds,
A legacy of hearts so bold.

Through whispered winds and silent cries,
Their courage lives, it never dies.
In paths they carved, through storm and sun,
Their journey's end, yet never done.

To follow where the legends tread,
Is to embolden heart and head.
To seek the truth, beyond the veil,
In every breath, their lore entail.

In the path of legends, find your stride,
Eternal lessons, as your guide.
Their spirit walks beside you still,
With every step, a pledge fulfilled.

Through Wind and Rain

In the harsh embrace of whispering gale,
Their hearts beat true, never frail.
Through wind and rain, they forge ahead,
With dreams that burn, brightly fed.

The tempest roars, its fearsome cry,
Yet through it all, they dare to fly.
Their spirits, like the morning mist,
In unity, their hopes persist.

Under skies of grey and thunder's roar,
Resilient souls, seek the shore.
In every storm, their strength is found,
Rooted deep, in faith profound.

With every gust, their voices rise,
A hymn of hope beneath the skies.
Through trials faced, and sorrows known,
In every drop, their courage shown.

Through wind and rain, they stand as one,
From darkest night to rising sun.
Their journey etched in nature's flow,
In steadfast hearts, their virtues glow.

Nature's Titan

Amidst the whispering pines, tall and grand,
Mountains rise where the sky does command,
The wind echoes through verdant canopies,
Nature's titan, braving endless seas.

Through valleys deep, where shadows play,
Sunlight dances in a gilded display,
Rivers carve paths in eternal embrace,
This land, a testament to time's grace.

Birdsong heralds the dawn anew,
In this sanctuary of green and blue,
The earth's heartbeat in every breeze,
Nature's titan, whisper to the trees.

Crowning peaks with alabaster snow,
Witness to where the wildflowers grow,
Timeless beauty etched in ancient stone,
Here lies a world of its own.

From summit heights to meadow's bend,
A story told with no end,
The whispers of the forest, nature's choir,
In every leaf, in every spire.

Unbroken Trails

Through fields of gold, we tread our path,
Unbroken trails of aftermath,
The journey calls with each new day,
Leading us, in its own way.

Beneath the canopy, shadows dance,
Whispers of the forest's trance,
Footsteps echo on the ancient ground,
Lost in the beauty we've found.

Each stone, each root, a story tells,
Of times gone by, of living wells,
The winding road under sky so vast,
Reflects the journeys of the past.

In twilight's glow, horizons near,
Chasing dreams, conquering fear,
Unbroken trails through heart and land,
Guiding visions, hand in hand.

With steadfast steps, we blaze anew,
Every vista brings a brighter view,
Through life's journeys, vast and tale,
We chart our course, unbroken trail.

Pride of the Prairie

Endless skies and waving grain,
Where freedom roams upon the plain,
Pride of the prairie, wide and free,
Nature's canvas, wild and sea.

Amber waves in the summer's sigh,
Underneath the boundless sky,
The whispers of the earth so pure,
In this heartland, we endure.

Horizon stretches far and wide,
On this expanse, the spirits ride,
Through seasons change, the cycles spin,
Prairie's pride, where dreams begin.

Thunder rolls and rivers weave,
Stories that the breezes leave,
Roots run deep in golden fields,
To the prairie's might, our spirit yields.

With every dawn, a fresh command,
Written by a timeless hand,
Pride of the prairie, strong and true,
In every heartbeat, me and you.

Echoes of Majesty

In forest deep and mountain high,
Echoes of majesty amplify,
Through ancient trees and whispered songs,
Nature's voice where soul belongs.

From timeworn cliffs to valley wide,
The echoes of greatness do reside,
In every rustle, stream's soft plea,
A symphony, wild and free.

Majesty of dawn's first light,
Painting skies in hues so bright,
The echoes call from dusk till dawn,
Nature's hymn on the breezes borne.

Within the stillness, shadows play,
Earth's secrets in the softest sway,
Every leaf and stone, a story,
Echoes of nature's timeless glory.

Footfalls on the forest's floor,
Silent vows from ages yore,
In whispers, roars, and silence sweet,
Echoes of majesty our hearts entreat.

Galloping Might

With hooves like thunder, hearts reconnect,
Through fields of green, no path select.
Beneath the sun, in strength they fight,
Nature's beasts, in galloping might.

Their manes like wind, in wild embrace,
In freedom's dance, no chains or trace.
Eyes of fire, spirits bright,
Echoes of the ancient night.

They break the dawn with fervent stride,
Melding dreams with endless pride.
Through time's expanse, a noble sight,
Charging forth with all their might.

Earth beneath them yields in sway,
Silent force through night and day.
Unbridled souls, against the light,
Majestic in their galloping might.

In sync with storms, at nature's core,
Legends rise and tales restore.
The wild and free, forever fight,
Living dreams of galloping might.

Grace in Motion

Whispering winds, with subtle grace,
They move as shadows, leave no trace.
A ballet of the earth's own notion,
Life displayed in purest motion.

Through forests deep, in twilight's hue,
They weave their dreams, so silent, true.
Each stride a marvel, no commotion,
The essence found in gentle motion.

Upon the plains, 'neath skies so wide,
Their tranquil forms in beauty glide.
Harmony with time's devotion,
The world beholds their seamless motion.

As stars do dance in heavens' sweep,
They roam where earth and sky do meet.
Beauty found in soft expression,
Nature's art in endless motion.

In timeles grace, they pave their way,
Within the dusk, through light of day.
Bound to earth, their sacred potion,
A life enshrined in graceful motion.

Heart of the Plains

In heartlands wide, where grasses sway,
They journey forth, both night and day.
Unyielding souls in vast terrains,
They roam the boundless heart of plains.

Beneath the sky, where eagles soar,
They find their path, horizons more.
With strength and will, their spirit reigns,
The steadfast heart that ties the plains.

Through storms they stride, through rain and sun,
United as the many, one.
No fetters bind, no fear restrains,
Resilient hearts beat through the plains.

Their legacy, in tales and lore,
Of those who walked this land before.
Everlasting, nature's veins,
In every beat, the heart of plains.

Where freedom calls, they heed the cry,
In open fields beneath the sky.
A testament to life's refrains,
The constant, pulsing heart of plains.

Whispers of Power

In silence deep, where shadows fall,
They whisper strength beyond recall.
With gentle might, they tower,
Nature breathes its whispers of power.

Each leaf a tale, each breeze a song,
In quiet grace, they move along.
Their presence felt in every hour,
The world enriched by whispers of power.

From mountaintops to ocean's edge,
They stand through time, a solemn pledge.
Unseen yet felt, through sun and shower,
Enduring whispers of pure power.

The ancient call from earth's own core,
A strength that lasts forevermore.
Unbroken spirit, each dawn, each hour,
Infinity in whispers of power.

In moments hushed, the truth reveals,
Through nature's pulse, the heart that feels.
The silent force, unseen, no cower,
Life defined by whispers of power.

Swift Rebellion

Whispers ignite the night, sparks in dark aeons,
Daring hearts, united in shadow, break dawn.
Echoes of freedom rise, with fervent defiance,
Unchained steps dance, a swift rebellion's alliance.

Through the hush of twilight, voices break free,
Breaching the chains of a stifled decree.
Stars blaze as banners in resilient eyes,
The flame of revolt paints the dawn skies.

Fault lines of fear tremble beneath our feet,
The swift rebellion, where injustice meets.
Torchlight and valor in a world reborn,
A tempest of change, swirling in reform.

With each rebel step, shadows slowly part,
Resistance pulses, in every fiery heart.
A symphony of whispers, a chorus so grand,
Swift rebellion sweeps across the land.

Legacy of courage, etched in the night,
In swift rebellion's wake, dawn's early light.
Bound not by chains, but by freedom's creed,
A new world rises, with audacious speed.

Windborne Titans

Borne upon the wind, titans of the sky,
Eternal guardians, watching from on high.
Majesty unfurls in their shadowy flight,
Windborne titans, defenders of the night.

Mountains bow down to their whispered might,
Silent sentinels, cloaked in twilight.
Their wings, like thunder, cut through the air,
Windborne titans, fierce and fair.

In the language of stars, their stories are spun,
Against the dawn's edge, 'neath the rising sun.
Their gaze sweeps the earth, from peak to plain,
Windborne titans, through the storm and rain.

Unseen they traverse through realms untamed,
Guarding the lands, where legends are named.
Their breath, a gale, over fields and seas,
Windborne titans, ruling with ease.

Ancient and wise, they soar without end,
On winds eternal, their might they lend.
In the heart of the storm, their secrets reside,
Windborne titans, our eternal guide.

Commanding Silence

In the hush before dawn, where shadows lie,
A commanding silence whispers through the sky.
Echoes of the night, in silence retained,
Each star a secret, carefully constrained.

The whisper of leaves in twilight's breath,
Commanding silence, defying death.
In the still of the night, a presence profound,
Quiet as a heartbeat, the silence resounds.

Mysteries shrouded in the calm of nigh,
Unveiling truths in a soft, silent sigh.
The moon's pale gaze, serenely just,
Commanding silence, in whispers of trust.

Upon the waves, where time ceases tread,
Silence reigns where words go unsaid.
In fields of thought, untouched by fear,
Commanding silence, crystal clear.

In every secret, the universe keeps,
A commanding silence, endless and deep.
Through the quiet, wisdom does tender,
In silence, we find all moments to remember.

Steady Ascent

Through peaks and valleys, the journey unfolds,
Each step measured, as the dawn grows bold.
In patient strides, where hopes ascend,
A steady ascent, till the very end.

Clouds part gently, revealing the way,
The mountains beckon, in the light of day.
Each breath a promise, each climb a creed,
Steady ascent, where dreams intercede.

Through storms and sunlight, we press to the crest,
With hearts unwavering, in relentless quest.
The path is rugged, the climb is steep,
A steady ascent, where spirits leap.

In whispers of winds, in echoes below,
The summit calls, with a radiant glow.
With faith as our guide, and courage as friend,
Steady ascent, towards heights that transcend.

At the peak's serene touch, the world sprawls wide,
The journey's whispers, the heart's silent guide.
In the symphony of the climb, our souls find rest,
Steady ascent, in the quest's gentle crest.

The Unbroken Soul

Among the shadows, gleams a light,
A beacon in the endless night.
Courage found in darkest hour,
Resilient heart, in full power.

A storm may batter, winds may howl,
Yet firmly stands, the unbroken soul.
Through trials faced, it only grows,
In strength and will, it ever glows.

The road is long, the path unclear,
But stride with faith, dispel the fear.
For deep within, the essence pure,
Unyielding spirit, bold and sure.

When mountains rise to block the way,
The unbroken soul shall never sway.
With every step, the scars may show,
Yet grace and strength, forever flow.

In life's great forge, the soul refined,
A diamond bright, with light aligned.
Unyielding, brave, through storm and flame,
The unbroken soul shall rise again.

Valiant Grace

Upon the fields of glory wide,
With purpose clear and hearts of pride.
They march with grace, the noble few,
In valor clad, both tried and true.

Their eyes alight with fiery gaze,
A steadfast will that none can faze.
In moments dire, they firmly stand,
With valiant grace, they take command.

No storm too fierce, no night too long,
For they uphold a courage strong.
In every trial, their spirits shine,
A valiant grace so pure, divine.

Oft battles rage, and chaos roars,
Yet through it all, their heart restores.
To lift the fallen, mend the break,
With valiant grace, for love's own sake.

And when the echoes fade away,
Under the sun's redeeming ray.
With heads held high, their deeds embrace,
The legacy of valiant grace.

Beneath the Saddle

Beneath the saddle, earth's embrace,
A journey shared, at measured pace.
Through valleys green and mountains tall,
Together, heed adventure's call.

The rhythmic beat of hooves on ground,
A symphony, a timeless sound.
Each stride a tale of trust and bond,
Beneath the saddle, hearts respond.

In dawn's first light or dusk's soft glow,
Through tempests fierce or gentle snow.
Companions true, through thick and thin,
Beneath the saddle, souls akin.

A whispered breeze, a quiet stream,
In silent moments, hopes and dreams.
The world expands, horizons wide,
Beneath the saddle, paths collide.

As miles unfold in endless dance,
The journey shared, a life's romance.
With every step, a story told,
Beneath the saddle, dreams unfold.

Iron Will

Through fires of trial, they forge their way,
An iron will that does not sway.
With heart of steel and mind aligned,
In battle fierce, the strength defined.

No mountain high or valley low,
Can break the spirit's endless glow.
With iron will, they push ahead,
Through darkest night, till dawn spreads.

In moments bleak, when shadows loom,
The iron will dispels the gloom.
Unyielding force, with courage bright,
They conquer fear and seize the light.

The path may twist, the journey hard,
Yet iron will remains unmarred.
In every clash and every test,
Their steadfast spirit shows its best.

So stand with pride, and march with pride,
Let iron will be your guide.
For in its strength, you'll find a way,
To rise, to shine, to seize the day.

Hooves of Thunder

Across the plains, where shadows roam,
The mighty steed calls this his home.
With every step, the earth does shake,
As hooves of thunder paths do make.

A mane of fire, eyes of flame,
Unleashed by none, too wild to tame.
Through storm and night, through field and dell,
A tale of power, he does tell.

Each stride, a testament to might,
A silhouette against the night.
The echoes in the canyon's deep,
Awaken those who dare to sleep.

When dawn's first light does paint the sky,
The hooves of thunder pass us by.
Unseen, yet felt, this force of nature,
A living, breathing wild creature.

So heed the call of distant sounds,
Where freedom's spirit fiercely bounds.
In every beat of hooves that thunder,
Lies the call to rise and wonder.

Wild Heart Unbridled

In twilight meadows, loosed and free,
A wild heart beats in harmony.
Against the wind, untamed and wild,
A spirit roams, nature's own child.

Boundless joy in every leap,
Through valleys wide and canyons steep.
No bond to hold, no chain to tie,
Wild heart's quest beneath the sky.

Gentle streams and rugged lands,
To all she whispers, understands.
Her breath, the breeze that stirs the dawn,
Her song, a legacy passed on.

In moonlit nights and sun's embrace,
This wild heart claims her rightful place.
Each pulse a story, unconfined,
A dance of life, both fierce and kind.

Her journey, one of endless flight,
A path of stars that burns so bright.
Unbridled, free, forever young,
A symphony yet to be sung.

Rider of Tempests

Through iron skies and raging storm,
There rides a figure, swift and warm.
With lightning's flash and thunder's call,
The rider of tempests conquers all.

With cloak of night and eyes of fire,
They journey forth, their heart's desire.
To tame the wild and fierce domain,
And dance amidst the wind and rain.

A roar of power, a surge of grace,
As storm clouds twist in wild embrace.
Each gale, a challenge to defy,
A testament to strength on high.

The rider's touch, both firm and light,
Commands the tempest's furious might.
In every gust, the whisper clear,
Of courage that disperses fear.

So when the heavens break apart,
Remember well this steadfast heart.
For in the storm's most furious cry,
The rider of tempests passes by.

Gale-Runner

Across the seas and endless sky,
Where eagles soar and spirits fly,
There runs a soul with wind at heel,
A whisper swift, a presence real.

In dawn's first breath and twilight's sigh,
The gale-runner races high.
Their path unseen, yet always known,
A current wild, forever flown.

With freedom's mark and courage strong,
They journey through the world's broad song.
A dance with fate, a bold decree,
Upon the air, forever free.

Their laughter mingles with the breeze,
Embracing life with utmost ease.
No anchor holds, no tether claims,
The wind-call runner knows no names.

So in the stillness, listen close,
To winds that tell a tale of those,
Who run the gales, unbound and true,
Eternal in their endless view.

Noble Steed's Resolve

Upon the moorland green and wide,
Where morning mists and shadows hide,
A gleam of strength in every stride,
The noble steed shall never bide.

In battles fierce and silent night,
With hooves that drum both dark and light,
To lands afar and peaks of might,
The noble steed holds fast the fight.

With spirit wild and eyes of flame,
No whisper ever speaks of shame,
Through tempest wild and world's acclaim,
The noble steed remains the same.

In meadows lush or fields of gray,
Through endless night and break of day,
With courage fierce, it keeps its way,
A symbol grand, none can betray.

From mountain high to valley low,
Its heart beats strong, its spirit grows,
A timeless tale the winds bestow,
The noble steed, forever shows.

Forge of Freedom

In fires old and anvils bright,
Where sparks of courage pierce the night,
The forge of freedom burns so bright,
A beacon in the endless fight.

With hands of steel and hearts so bold,
The tale of freedom's fight is told,
In each new blade, and iron mold,
A truth that never shall grow old.

'Tis not just iron, not just flame,
But values deep within the frame,
The forge of freedom never tame,
A dance of hope in freedom's name.

Through hardship's breath and toil's rest,
With every challenge sternly pressed,
The forge of freedom holds its quest,
To shape a future truly blessed.

From distant past to times unknown,
Its legacy in hearts is sown,
In every spark and tempered tone,
A world where freedom's spirit's grown.

Wild Dominion

In forests dense where shadows play,
And whispers of the wild convey,
A realm of life both night and day,
The wild dominion holds its sway.

Upon the peaks where eagles soar,
Where mountain streams in silence roar,
The spirit of the untamed core,
In wild dominion, forevermore.

Through desert sands and ocean wide,
The wild its secrets cannot hide,
In every leaf, and every tide,
The wild dominion shall abide.

Beneath the stars in velvet sky,
Where howls of wolves and loons' cry,
A symphony that never dies,
The wild dominion's lullaby.

Yet in its vast and boundless grace,
Is found a power none can chase,
A truth that time cannot erase,
The wild dominion sets its pace.

Hooves of Valor

On fields where silence speaks of war,
Where echoes of the past implore,
The hooves of valor, ever more,
In courage's name they stomp the floor.

Through storm and strife, through earth and flame,
In battles fierce where honor's claimed,
The hooves of valor, none can tame,
Through every fear, they stake their name.

With pulse of earth and spirit grand,
They charge where none can firmly stand,
The hooves of valor, bold they brand,
A legacy across the land.

In whispers soft of ancient lore,
Where shields were raised and banners tore,
The hooves of valor, to the core,
Remind us what we're fighting for.

In peace they walk, in war they fly,
With heartbeats strong beneath the sky,
The hooves of valor never shy,
In every hoofbeat, dreams run high.

Horizon Chaser

The horizon calls, a beckoning light,
Where day meets dusk in colors bright.
Footsteps echo on paths unknown,
Chasing dreams, where winds have flown.

Mountains loom with shadows grand,
Rivers carve their tracks in sand.
Skies arrayed in twilight's hue,
Guide the soul, to journeys new.

Stars emerge in the silent sky,
Whispers of a world nearby.
Each horizon, a tale to weave,
For those who wander and believe.

Fields of gold, and forests deep,
Guard the secrets that they keep.
Awake the chaser in the night,
With heart's desire as guiding light.

Through mist and moss, on endless quest,
To find the place where dreams do rest.
The horizon whispers ever near,
To those who chase without fear.

Spirit of the Meadows

Beneath the skies where wildflowers sway,
The spirit of the meadows plays.
In fields of green and petals pure,
Lives the magic, ancient and sure.

Breezes carry songs of old,
Stories in the blossoms fold.
Whispered secrets on the breeze,
Speak of timeless, gentle ease.

Sunlit paths through grassy seas,
Lead to realms of dreams and peace.
Nature's hymns, so soft and sweet,
Guide the steps of wandering feet.

Morning dew and evening glow,
Paint a world where spirits flow.
In each corner, life abounds,
In the meadows' sacred grounds.

As dusk descends in hues of gold,
The spirit's tales are proudly told.
In the heart of every bloom,
Lies the meadow's living room.

Thunderous Elegance

Sky in turmoil, tempest's cry,
Thunder's voice declares the sky.
Lightning's dance, a fierce embrace,
In nature's wild and wondrous place.

Raindrops fall with measured grace,
On fields and streams, each leaves a trace.
The storm's grand symphony resounds,
In the electric night, it bounds.

Winds that howl and shadows leap,
Through the vale, the spirits sweep.
Clouds that rove in dark parades,
Cast their spells in fleeting shades.

The storm, a painter in the storm,
Creates its art in vivid form.
Thunder taps the earth and sea,
With elegance, fierce and free.

When silence follows, skies renew,
A calm descends in silver hue.
Nature's elegance, thunderous and bright,
Fades into the arms of night.

Crest of Might

Upon the peak where eagles soar,
Stands the crest of legends' lore.
Mighty rocks and skies so vast,
Guard the memories of the past.

Winds ascend with whispers proud,
Brushing cliffs and mountain shroud.
Each step a testament of will,
To reach the heights, to climb the hill.

Above the clouds, where silence reigns,
Strength in solitude remains.
Echoes of the earth below,
Tell of battles long ago.

Snow that crowns the rugged face,
Reflects a timeless, sacred grace.
The crest, a temple to behold,
In its arms, the brave and bold.

By dawn's light and twilight's kiss,
Mountains wear a veil of bliss.
Crest of might, where spirits soar,
Guard the tales, forever more.

Roaring Equestrian

Hooves thundering across the plains,
A symphony of strength unchained,
Dust rising in a mighty surge,
With every stride, the wild emerge.

Manes billow like a stormy sea,
Eyes aflame with fierce decree,
In unity, they seek their quest,
A testament to nature's best.

Hearts pounding with unyielding grace,
In every step, a noble trace,
Bound by sky and earth they reign,
In sunlight's glow and tempest's gain.

Unbridled spirits run their course,
An untamed, relentless force,
Roaring, like the winds of old,
Their stories in each hoofbeat told.

Unwritten paths beneath their tread,
To freedom's call, they have been led,
Roaring equestrian, wild and free,
A timeless dance, epitome.

Fabled Gallop

In twilight's glow, they make their mark,
Ghostly forms in shadows stark,
Through ages past, a legend born,
A gallop fabled, lone and worn.

Whispers of a bygone might,
Carved in tales by campfire light,
Galloping 'neath the moon's cool gleam,
Enshrined within each dream.

Endurance weaves through every race,
An echo of a bygone grace,
With hooves that drum the earth below,
In every beat, a hero's flow.

Their spirits bound by unseen ties,
A saga drawn in endless skies,
Galloping past horizons wide,
Eternal as the rising tide.

Fabled gallopers, strong and pure,
Through legends, they forever endure,
In every stride, a tale they weave,
Immortal lives, as we believe.

Mountain's Pride

Upon the ridge, where winds unite,
Stand beings of majestic might,
The mountains watch, a silent guide,
With every stream, their hearts confide.

Clad in peaks of icy crown,
In valleys where great streams come down,
Sturdy souls with eyes of fire,
To heights, their spirits long aspire.

Braced against the tempest's roar,
Their legacy forevermore,
Each echo of their mighty call,
Carries tales of fall and thrall.

With hooves that trace the jagged stone,
They carve a path through worlds unknown,
Mountain's pride, in twilight's grace,
Upholding past in steadfast chase.

Through mists and dawns, they take their flight,
Guardians of the morning light,
In silence, they command the land,
Mountain's pride, forever grand.

Brave and Unbroken

Through fields of gold, they race in glee,
Born to roam eternally,
With eyes that gleam like stars at night,
Brave and unbroken in their flight.

Chasing dreams across the plains,
Unfettered by the earthly chains,
Each heartbeat sings a freedom's song,
In every stride, they smile along.

Where pastures blend with endless sky,
They conquer realms, no bounds defy,
Strong, resilient, unconfined,
To fate's embrace, they leave behind.

An emblem of endurance shown,
In every trial, they've grown,
Unyielding to the storms they face,
An epitome of boundless grace.

Brave and unbroken, they remain,
Through sunlit fields and autumn rain,
Eternal symbols of the free,
In their gallop, infinity.

Guardian of the Range

Beneath the endless sky so wide,
Where wind and earth in dance reside,
The guardian stands, a noble sight,
Protecting all from dawn till night.

His shadow falls on verdant land,
A steely gaze, a guiding hand,
Through storm and sun, through dusk and dawn,
He holds the range, forever strong.

The wild ones run, the rivers bend,
But he remains, a constant friend,
With heart so fierce and spirit bold,
The guardian, a tale retold.

In whispered winds, his name survives,
Through ancient tales, his legend thrives,
For he shall guard, by night and day,
On endless range, where spirits play.

The stars above know all his deeds,
In silent nights, the land he feeds,
A beacon bright, a watchful eye,
The guardian of the range stands nigh.

Tenacity in Motion

Against the tide, through wave and wind,
The heart persists, it won't rescind,
For in each pulse, the spirit roars,
Tenacity in motion soars.

The mountain's height, the valley low,
Through trials fierce, through endless woe,
A force unyielding, never still,
With iron will, it climbs the hill.

Through darkest night, through blinding light,
Unfazed by fear, undimmed by plight,
Onward it moves, through storm and grace,
Each challenge met with steadfast pace.

The world may turn, the seasons change,
Yet it moves forth, both near and strange,
With every step, a louder beat,
In rhythm with the earth's heartbeat.

Unknown the end, unseen the goal,
But onward drives the restless soul,
Tenacity, in motion bound,
A force of nature, all around.

Desert Mirage

In scorching sun, where shadows play,
A vision shimmers miles away,
A fleeting dream, a wisp of cheer,
The desert mirage, bright and clear.

Golden dunes stretch far and wide,
Beneath the azure sky they bide,
And in the shimmering, wavering air,
Illusions form, a land so fair.

Oasis gleams with verdant trees,
A trick of mind, as hot winds tease,
Cool waters call, a promise sweet,
Yet fade away beneath the heat.

Travelers lost in endless sand,
Reach out for dreams just out of hand,
For in this vast, unyielding space,
Mirages form, then leave no trace.

The desert holds its ancient lore,
A land of myths and so much more,
Where dreams may live and quickly fade,
In mirage, softly cast and laid.

Unconquered Steed

Beneath a sky of endless blue,
A steed of night, in shadowed hue,
With spirit fierce and eyes so bright,
It roams the wild, a living light.

No reins can hold, no bridle tame,
A force of nature, free of shame,
With mane that dances in the breeze,
It gallops swift among the trees.

Against the wind, it strides alone,
In open fields it finds its home,
Unbridled strength and heart so vast,
A legend born, a story cast.

Through moonlit nights and sunlit days,
It travels on in boundless ways,
Unconquered by the hand of man,
This steed runs free across the land.

With every stride, it clears the air,
A symbol wild, beyond compare,
An unconquered steed, forever free,
In timeless dance with destiny.

Indomitable Rush

Through valleys deep, where shadows creep,
A river's song begins its leap,
With currents fierce, it carves its path,
Indomitable strength, it hath.

Stones erode, yet still it flows,
An endless dance, through highs and lows,
Whispers of life in every drop,
It knows no end, it shall not stop.

Mountains tall that flank its side,
Can't tame the spirit in its stride,
Boundless vigor, wild and free,
A testament to what can be.

Sweeping through the forests dense,
Breaking through all resistance,
With every surge, it finds its course,
Relentless, driven by unseen force.

Echoes of the ancient streams,
It carries forth our hopes and dreams,
Indomitable rush, through time and space,
Eternal power, nature's grace.

Guardian of the Pastures

Beneath the sun's embrace so warm,
Lies the keeper of this land's charm,
Green fields stretching far and wide,
In their beauty, peace does abide.

Gentle giant with watchful eye,
Underneath the azure sky,
Guardian of the pastures fair,
Protects with tender, loving care.

Soft whisper of the morning breeze,
Rustling through the ancient trees,
In the meadows calm and still,
His presence felt on every hill.

Cows and sheep in quiet graze,
Beneath his gaze, through sunlit haze,
Nature's shepherd, steadfast and true,
Guiding all as the day is new.

Endless green and whispering gold,
Stories of the past retold,
Guardian of the pastures bright,
Holding all within his sight.

Herald of Dawn

In the hush before the light,
Whispers of the coming bright,
Night surrenders to the morn,
This is when the day is born.

Golden rays that pierce the dark,
Songs of birds, a welcome spark,
The herald of dawn, with gentle grace,
Brings new hope to every place.

Mist retreats with fleeting dreams,
Over hills and flowing streams,
A symphony of colors seen,
In the early morning sheen.

Silent stars fade from the sky,
Their watch concluded with a sigh,
As day breaks with a tender kiss,
Lending peace and newfound bliss.

Moments pure, the world awakes,
In this light, the heart partakes,
Herald of dawn, a promise true,
Life begins, in mornings hue.

Field Commander

Strong and resolute he stands,
Guiding troops with steady hands,
In fields where battles forge and rage,
He writes history, page by page.

Armor gleaming in the sun,
Leading till the fight is won,
With strategies both bold and wise,
Victory he seeks, through sacrifice.

Echoes of commands so clear,
Instilling strength, dispelling fear,
Field commander, brave and strong,
In his courage, hearts belong.

Banners high and spirits rise,
Beneath his watch, the future lies,
Through every trial, every pain,
He ensures it's not in vain.

Legends born of steadfast will,
The clash of titans, echoes still,
Field commander, in the fray,
Guides his forces, leads the way.

Milton Keynes UK
Ingram Content Group UK Ltd.
UKHW022239280824
447491UK00010B/283